Life After Mississippi

by

James A. Autry

Introduction by Willie Morris

Photography by Lola Mae Autry

Yoknapatawpha Press
OXFORD, MISSISSIPPI

Also by James A. Autry:
Nights Under a Tin Roof

Published by Yoknapatawpha Press
P.O. Box 248, Oxford, MS 38655

Copyright © 1989 by James A. Autry
Note: The following poems appeared previously in *Kentucky Poetry Review:*
"Goodbye Truck Stop Girls" (Spring, 1985), and "Examining the Wreckage"
(Fall, 1987).

Library of Congress Catalogue Card Number 89-51148

ISBN 0-916242-59-5

Printed in the United States of America

Book and cover design by Lawrence Wells

to Sally...
...for whom I am thankful every single day

CONTENTS

◆ ◆ ◆

ACKNOWLEDGMENTS AND THANKS

Knowing where to begin is the hard part of writing acknowledgments. So many people played some part in this book or in my life, or both, that I cannot possibly name them all. Nor would naming them pay the proper tribute for all they have done.

Rather than apologize further for what I can't do, however, let me do what I can.

First, I thank my wife, friend, and critic, Sally, to whom this book is dedicated.

Next, I thank my sons: Jim, who in resisting all the pressures of the past 18 months, has taught me much about courage; Rick, who in living his life as if he had no handicap at all, has taught me much about the much-maligned power of optimism; and Ronald, who in his five blessed years of life, has taught me much about patience and trying to live in the grace of each moment. All three sons are woven throughout several poems in this book.

I thank my stepmother, Lola Mae Autry, for her wonderful photographs. What started as a way to illustrate my father's articles has become an almost full-time profession for her. It should be said that many of these photos have required her best darkroom skills in restoration and printing of some very old "box-camera" snapshots. These pictures are not intended as specific illustrations for the poems; rather they are their own expression of a time and place.

And I thank my Mississippi family, brother Lanny and sister Martha Lynn and their families, Deborah and Susan and Amy, and Ray and Clint.

My cousin Douglas has been a constant friend and inspiration to me for many years. His wife, Elizabeth, is among the most abiding and supportive people on earth. They have consistently nurtured me with their generous spirits.

And I must acknowledge the people of the Abel's Store community and Pine Grove Church. They and their kin appear throughout my poetry, but as I tell them when I visit: "Don't try to figure out who's who in these poems; I've moved the facts around, and only the truth remains."

Also a part of this book and of my life are my sister-in-law Susie, widow of my brother, and her children, Susan and John, and their families.

And I thank my publishers, Larry and Dean Wells, who took the leap in publishing my first book in 1983. I thank them for their confidence, and I thank them for continuing to run a high-quality regional press in the face of today's business pressures.

Finally, I thank you, the readers who responded so enthusiastically to "Nights Under a Tin Roof." It was your support that led directly to the publishing of this book.

◆ ◆ ◆

J.A.A.
Des Moines, Iowa
May 4, 1989

INTRODUCTION
by
Willie Morris

Jim Autry and I have many things in common. We both grew up in Mississippi, then went away from it to work in the magazine trade, to write and to edit other people's writings. What we share most strongly, however, is a regard for our native ground, for the people and traditions there.

Jim was raised in the hill country of North Mississippi, in Benton County. I consider myself a flatlander, having grown up in Yazoo City, where the hills meet the delta. My people always sympathized with the folks "up north in those hills" who had to wrench a living out of hard ground. Yet we had an inordinate respect for the hill people's endurance and strength, their tenacious religion and friendships and family ties that seemed as tough as the rocky land that spawned them.

These are the qualities that I sense in my friend, Jim Autry, both the man and the poet. In his distinguished verse he shares with us the power of his faith in mankind, his sense of community in the face of adversity. He takes us back and forth between the past and present, between the youth that we remember and the future we face together. His poems reflect the lessons life teaches: "Grabblin' " is about rites of passage, about where courage comes from; "Flavors" reminds us of youth and innocence and the simple joy of being; "Fishing Day" takes us back in a rush to the great Mississippi outdoors; "Ordination" is about change, about new beginnings.

Life After Mississippi is Autry's tribute to his Mississippi roots, to the places and people that nurtured him and which now sustain him in the corporate boardrooms of America, in anonymous, scented hotel rooms, on 747 flights from New York to L.A. while he sits strapped in his seat writing about half-forgotten funerals in country churchyards. As a successful executive he keeps his mind on his work but his heart, as they say, is down home.

> *Yet it is with me still*
> *in the fall smell of wood smoke*
> *from some suburban chimney,*
> *in an Atlanta taxi driver's turn of phrase,*
> *in the quiet of an old church in Bavaria...*

For what Autry is writing about, again and again, is home. He listens to voices heard and unheard, and he touches something deep in our hearts. He is an observer whose task it is to remind us of those small but important details that add up to a significant understanding.

"Life," he writes, "is largely a matter of paying attention."

◆ ◆ ◆

I. Mississippi

· · ·

Fishing Day

I

Old ladies in bonnets fished
with cane poles,
baiting their hooks with worms
or grubs from under a wet log
turned over by one of us boys.
They sat,
long sleeved against the mosquitos
and watched cork bobbers
and caught small bream,

> *Lord, they are the sweetest little fish.*
> *Fry 'em crispy and eat 'em*
> *bones and all*

tossing them in a bucket
where they splashed and swam a while
then turned belly up,
their gills moving in and out
slowly until they died.

II

We would go to the bottom early,
in a mule wagon,
men and boys and women and girls
and babies and dogs and all,
and the men and boys would find
a flat dry place
and start fires and cut green brush,

> *Build up a little smoke, boys,*
> *keep them skeeters away*

and the women and girls would spread quilts
and sometimes make a mosquito net tent
for the babies
but most times would just fan them,
or we'd build shelters of branches
if it looked like a sprinkle,
and always a big cooking fire.
We brought flour sacks and tow sacks
full of iron skillets
and salt and corn meal and lard.
We brought plates and knives and forks and glasses.
There were gallon jugs of tea
and always cakes and pies.

III

But we couldn't eat until we caught fish,
not little bream but catfish,
blues and willows and yellows and channels,
on set hooks.
First some of us cut saplings or cane
then trimmed and sharpened the ends
while others seined for bait
in the little sloughs and backwaters
left from when the river flooded.

> *You boys watch for cottonmouths,*
> *they like them sloughs.*

Then we'd unroll our hooks
one at a time,
big claw hooks on heavy cotton cord
with nuts and washers and whatever else
for weight,
and tie them to the poles.
Under a low-hanging tree was good
or the downstream side of a log
or around a drift,

> *Mind you don't set so close in there,*
> *he'll hang you on a branch and slip away*

jamming the sharpened end of the pole
deep into the mud bank,

> *Stick it deep, boys.*
> *I lost a pole one time that was a foot*
> *in the bank. Pulled it out and swam off.*

then pushing the pole down parallel to the water
until the hook touched bottom
and the line bowed,
then up just a few inches.

> *Come and get it, Mr. Catfish.*

IV

When we had set maybe a hundred hooks
we seined more bait,
then we ran the hooks,
moving along the slick bank,
checking each hook, rebaiting,
always hoping the next pole
would be jerking,
slapping the water,
then arguing over whose turn it was
to land the fish.

V

The women who did not fish sat on quilts
and fanned with palm leaf
or funeral parlor fans
and talked about the heat
or the mosquitos or something they heard at church.
And they yelled at the children
to stay back from the bank.

> *You slide in that water*
> *we'll never see you again.*

And sometimes one might sing a church song
while the others listened or hummed,
and one might do some sewing,

> *I swear, Nora, you make*
> *the straightest little stitches.*

and they would watch
how the fishing was going
and tend the cooking fire
until the coals were right.

VI

The men never wanted to eat
because they came to fish
but the little children would get fussy
and the women would spread a place,

> *Boys, better clean some of them fish*

and we would punch a hole
at the back of the catfish's head
and run a broom straw down his backbone,

> *Paralyzes 'em.*

then cut the skin enough to grab it with pliers
and pull it right down to his tail,
first breaking his fins at the base.

> *Git them fins before they git you.*

With a big one,
at least ten pounds,
we'd nail him to a tree,
through the head,
then make the cut and skin him.
The guts were a mess
but we kept some parts for bait,

the only fun of it
seeing what was in his stomach.
You'd be surprised what we found sometimes,
a whole turtle, shell and all,
a little snake,
one time a mouse,
and the girls hated it.

VII

The women would roll catfish steaks
in corn meal
then put them in a skillet of hot lard,
with sliced potatoes in another,
and hushpuppies after the fish,
and the girls would get out the slaw and tea.

> *Boys run git the men*
> *and tell 'em we're ready*
> *for the blessing.*

And we would bow our heads
while a deacon gave thanks
for the day and the fish
and the fellowship,
and blessed the food to the good
of our bodies, amen.

VIII

In the afternoon there were naps
and more fishing
and quiet talking
and sometimes a rain shower
which nobody minded
and which usually made the fish bite better,

> *Look at 'em. They're loading on.*

all of us wondering why that was.
Then we'd begin to load the wagon,
the men arguing about
whether to take up the lines
or bait them overnight
and come back in the morning.
We always left the hooks
because no one could resist the possibility
of coming tomorrow and finding
a pole bent into the water
straining against the biggest catfish
we would ever see.

◆ ◆ ◆

Mister Mac

People didn't know how to take Mister Mac,
"whippoorwill" they called him
because his nose made him look like one,
and laughed when he ran,
the only Republican in the county.

> *Feel we need a two-party system.*

Still, something was sad about his twenty or so votes,
though he said it was more
than he had family,

> *Musta convinced a few.*

and went on about his business,
writing insurance
for companies who wished
they could get someone else,
but nobody in the territory
wanted to bump Mister Mac
out of the job,
his being the only support for his sisters,
and most of the people having gone to school to him
at one time or another,
back when he was one of the few educated men
in the area,
though even then they didn't know whether to admire
or feel sorry for him
because it was not easy to be educated
and amount to much in those days.
So they called him whippoorwill
and dodged his car
when he drove, cataracts and all,
to the square,
where he would soften them up
with humor,

> *You never been choked*
> *till you been choked on a sweet tater.*

then tell all who would listen
how the South would never rise again
without a two-party system,
ending with his favorite story.

One time the judge asked this man,
"Henry, what you got to say
before I sentence you to hang
by the neck till dead?"
Henry said, "Judge, I just
want to say it sure is gonna
be a lesson to me."

But "peculiar" was the word they used,
not eccentric, like nowadays;
"kinda peculiar," they'd say.
Mister Mac thought they admired his spunk
despite how they treated him,

Trying their best not to listen,
they hear me though.

but when he died and his cousin sobbed
all through the service
and told me, "Jimmy there's not a dry eye
in this town today,"
the preacher had to ask the people
to bunch up in the front
so it would look like a crowd.

◆ ◆ ◆

Cousin El

When I remember my childhood Mississippi
I think of Cousin El
who lost his sight to a sweet gum ball
and lived the rest of life on the home place.
Did he always see those hills and fields and trees
as they were when he was a child
throwing sweet gum balls with his brothers?
And will I always see that place
as it was,
sweet and green and dusty,
and not as it is now,
a kind of blindness protecting me
from the video stores and pizza shops
and straightened rivers
and thinned forests?

The answers are yes and yes,
but here's the difference:
I indulge the blindness,
and Cousin El would have loved to see the changes,
ugliness and all.

◆ ◆ ◆

Grabblin'

The word is grappling
but we said grabblin'
and bragged that Mississippi
was the only state with a season for it,
our real boast being that Mississippi
was the only state
with men and boys brave enough to do it,
to crouch in the water
and reach up under the bank,
bare-handed,
searching a slick hole
hoping for a catfish
and not a snake or snapper or dogfish
or any of the dangers
we knew could be under those waters.

II

We went in big groups,

> Don't ever grabble by yourself, boys,
> a 15-pound catfish can drown you.
> He's got you much as you got him.

six or eight men and that many boys,
in overalls and barefoot
or wearing our most wore-out shoes,
starting miles up the river
and wading the shallows,
which was most of it,
dropping into holes here and there,
waist or shoulder deep,
to poke around sunken logs or drifts
or under the mud banks.

III

Every boy had to catch a catfish,
sticking a thumb in the sandpaper mouth
and fingers in the gills,
pulling him from his den
where the precious eggs lay.

Be sure you got those gills
or he'll spin on your thumb
and peel the skin like a onion.

We'd put our catch in big tow sacks
dragging them behind us in the water
and when we rested we'd open the sacks
and tell our stories

That there jughead
got a piece of my thumb.

remembering each fish and its part of the river.
Grabblin' was for big fish
and we caught twenty- and thirty-pounders,
sometimes two men wrestling one
onto the bank
then resting out of breath
at the work of it.

IV

There may have been a thousand snakebites
and there may have been none;
though we boys expected snakes in every hole
our fear of shame was stronger than our fear of snakes.

Stick your hand on in there, boys,
a snake'll run from you,
you couldn't touch one if you tried.

We saw so many on the bank
and dropping from tree limbs as we moved toward them
that we held our breath
every time we reached into a hole
or we pretended to talk to the fish
the way the men did

Okay, Mr. Catfish, I need me something
to make the gravy stink tonight.

V

Sometimes a grabblin' would end
with a fish fry or big stew,
the women and girls gathering with all the food,
except fish,
in Ira's pasture where we would wade
out of the river
and dump our sacks onto the grass.

Then we'd clean fish
and change clothes
and show our blooded thumbs
to the little boys
and the girls,
telling them yes we saw snakes
but you can't worry about stuff like that
if you want to be a grabbler.

◆ ◆ ◆

When Boys Wanted To Go To War

When I sneaked the flashlight under the covers
and read comics
until the precious batteries were weak,
I learned all how to hate my enemies.

First
on those pages
with the shadow pictures of babies on bayonets
with their mothers looking terrified
while demonic Nazis and Japs
prepared to stick their gleaming daggers
you know where,
with the Nazi pilots
shouting, "Die you swine,"
as they machine-gunnned our pilots
parachuting from their burning
Lightnings or Mustangs or Spitfires.

Then
in church where
someone's son or brother was dead
and there was no turning the other cheek.

And
in a dozen hot red dust cemeteries
with honor guards and seven-gun salutes
making the babies wake and cry,
where there were little brothers itching
to grab those honor guard rifles
and load them with real bullets
and go get those dirty murderers.

And some little brothers did go
and some were too young
but went to Boy Scouts
and did close order drill like the army,
and hoped the war would last a long time.

◆ ◆ ◆

II. Leaving Mississippi

• • •

Leaving Mississippi

Part of me never left
and another part is always leaving,
leaving Mississippi but never gone.
"Jimmy when you gonna come on back
down home," my people ask,
and I cannot say, "Never,
I've found my home somewhere else"
any more than I can say my home
was never in the State of Mississippi
but in the community of it,
in my father's churches,
in Abel's store,
in Ashland on the square,
in how the people were together.
Now that home is gone forever from Mississippi—
yet it is with me still,
in the fall smell of wood smoke
from some suburban chimney,
in an Atlanta taxi driver's turn of phrase,
in the quiet of an old church in Bavaria,
in the call of an Iowa night hawk,
in a fish breaking the surface of a Colorado stream,
in the night peepers everywhere
in a stanza of Amazing Grace,
in the crickets,
in dust.

◆ ◆ ◆

Saying Goodbye

Every time I say goodbye to the old folks
I know it may be the last time,
and when it turns out to be,
I am still surprised
and regret the things I did not say,
so now I machine-gun the news to them,
everything I said at the past goodbye
and will say at the next one,
as if loading them with stories
and recollections
to take along
if they go before I return.

Yet I know I still will regret
the things I did not say,
the words that would cloud us up
and make us look at our shoes
and cause one of them to say,
"Aw save that talk till they're ready
to put me in the ground."

So I keep those words to myself,
not wanting anyone to think
I see death coming.

◆ ◆ ◆

"Your Uncle Vee Had A Massive Stroke Last Night"

June 23, 1987

Poem 1.

I always throw the number away
as if I'll never need it again,
then comes a call
and I dial the old 601-555-1212
and ask for Tippah County Hospital,
hearing those seven digits I've heard so often,
then punching the buttons,
dreading the voices,
dreading the things that won't be said.

Poem 2.

Uncle Vee is the last one now,
and I wonder if he's the only man in Mississippi
who still lives in a house he built
of raw lumber sixty years ago,
who plowed a mule in red clay,
over and around hills,
not a flat spot on the place,
who cursed crows in the garden
and hawks and foxes and chicken snakes,
who killed hogs and cured meat and smoked it,
who ate pork and greens and cornbread,
and drank gallons of buttermilk,
and got bigger and bigger
but at eighty-six was still hungry every day,
who taught six grades in the same red schoolhouse
before it was blown to bits by the Second Army
on maneuvers in Holly Springs National Forest,
who taught singing school
and led the choir
and took busloads of singers
to singing conventions all around five counties,
who served in the legislature
where he wore a tie every day,
and who was cheated out of the election
by a kind of politics he thought was a sin.

Poem 3.

Now Uncle Vee wants to go home,
he wants to sing hymns,
he wants to feel a plow breaking the ground,
he wants to drive his old car to the store
and talk about the weather
and buy somebody a belly washer
and smell the hoop cheese and coal oil.
He wants to see his wife
ironing in her straight wash dress,
wiping sweat with the back of her hand.
He wants to smell her biscuits
and put a dipper in the sweet water
she brings from the cistern.
He wants to hear his children
playing around the porch.
So he tries,
he wakes and pulls at the tubes
when the nurses aren't looking,
and cries when finally I reach him
on the telephone.

◆ ◆ ◆

Mortality

It's my turn to become my father,
liver spots, knotty hands and all,
time for me to tell my stories so many times
that someone thinks he should tape-record them
for his grandchildren
who will never know me.
Verdell is already his father
and I have heard his stories
of Calhoun and Leroy and Jimmie Lee
and I have turned on the tape recorder,
a sure sign.

◆ ◆ ◆

Flavors

It happened again
this time with blackberry jelly and bacon,
together like a cold morning
in Mississippi,
the fire popping and someone stamping his feet,
and troves of warmth here and there,
in front of the fireplace, around the kitchen stove,
from a bed with the covers thrown back.

It happened this time in one of those places
with toasted white bread
and grilled bacon cured with a needle
instead of in a smokehouse,
and Knott's Berry Farm blackberry preserves
from a one-serving jar,
even an orchid on the table.

Yet I could squint at those far from home palm trees,
and despite the china and crystal,
my pressed cuffs, dry-blown hair and Old-Spice smell,
could squeeze the blackberry and bacon
between my tongue and the roof of my mouth,
tasting and tasting,
all the old flavors again.

◆ ◆ ◆

Ordination

for the Rev. Ms. Patricia Ryan

Brother Jim Thompson came,
the oldest,
with overalls and a white shirt buttoned at the collar,
with a walking cane and a Bible
that had stood fifty years of pounding,
and with that old fire burning through his cataracts.

> *Didn't need no seminary.*
> *Always preached the Bible*
> *and the Lord Jesus Christ*
> *crucified and buried and*
> *raised from the dead.*

Brother Hamer came
and Brother Ewart
and the three Walker boys,
preachers all.
They came through rain,
wrestling the wheels of their out-of-county cars,
sliding in ruts so deep the tail pipes dragged.
They parked under the trees
and along the road,
then walked, shined shoes and all,
through the mud,
picking their way along the high spots
like children jumping puddles.
Into the church of their fathers,
the place they had all felt the call,
the old home church
where thousands of hands had pressed
on the bowed heads of new preacher boys,
of sun-reddened young men called by the Lord,
called from the cotton fields to preach the word.
They had felt the hands,
these old preachers,
felt those blunt-fingered, work-hardened hands,
felt them like a blessing,
like an offering,
like a burden.
Felt them at weddings and baptizings,
felt them in the heat of a summer revival sermon,
in the agony of a baby's funeral,
in the desperate prayer against some killer disease,
in the frustrating visit with a mind gone senile.

And now the old preachers come to lay their hands
on the head of a new kind of preacher,
a preacher from the seminary,
a preacher who studied the Bible in Greek and Hebrew,
who knew about religions they never heard of,
who knew about computers
and memory banks full of sermons
and many other modern things.
A new kind of preacher,
and yet,
a preacher who still would feel on her head
the hands
like a commandment
from all the preachers and deacons who ever were.

◆ ◆ ◆

Goodbye Truck Stop Girls

I

There was one not far from New Albany
named Velma
who could do the dirty boogie on one foot
all the way to the floor and up again
if you would feed the jukebox
and her pocket.

And there were others
named Mavis and Erlene and Wilma
and Inez and Bettyanne
and Lottie Sue and Sarah Vee
and they could all boogie and jitterbug
and wait tables at the same time
and take care of themselves
no matter what anybody said.

And the ones who didn't marry some old boy
and have babies
to bring back and show off
to the cooks and cashiers and other girls
got older and meaner
and started using coarse words
when we would feed the juke
and warned the younger girls about us
and then went on to do whatever they do
always in another town.

II

But something happened:
the juke music changed
and good old boys became cowboys
and the truck stop girls put on tight jeans
and cowboy boots
and talked about snorting toot
and asked the truck cowboys for bennies
and yellowjackets and stuff we never heard of

and broke out in a bunch of names
like Debbie and Lynn and Tammie
and Dawn and Renae
and Tanya and Crystal
and squealed into CB radios
for cowboys to stop in
and would hardly wait on anybody
and would never dance to the juke
no matter how many quarters we pumped.

◆ ◆ ◆

Television And The Church

Every time I find myself in the little church
where my grandfather and father
preached,
where my uncle led singing conventions
while someone played an upright piano
and pumped an old organ;
every time I feel the air-conditioning
and hear the latest hit
from the Top Forty Christian Countdown,
I think,
Damn you, television.

◆ ◆ ◆

Mississippi Writers Day

The irony was lost on no one.
There we sat,
poets, writers, teachers, scholars,
in the chamber where some
of our grandfathers and great-grandfathers
deliberated on how to solve
the nigra problem,
then passed the poll tax
and set up separate but equal schools
and decided that everyone had to read
and understand the constitution
before he could vote.
We sat there,
in the chamber in the building
whose bricks were made by slaves.
We sat and listened
to black poets,
to angry black poets
who read their words
so that no one could ever feel safe
reading them in a white voice.

It was a lesson about words
and how their color changes.
It was a lesson about places
and how their power changes.
It was a lesson about people
and how their fear changes.

◆ ◆ ◆

Elegy For A Gentle Person

She was sitting on the porch
in a cane bottom chair
leaning against the wall by the front door
watching them shoot blanks at the red schoolhouse
and throw smoke bombs through its windows,
her daddy shaking his head and cursing,

> *Reckon we'll win this war*
> *if the Japs hole up in a schoolhouse*

when the soldier came around the cistern
and stole her heart
just like in the stories.
Later, some said he was ignorant and worthless,
a lazy no count,
and she was the only one surprised
when he left after the children were born.
But back then he was handsome
in the uniform
and even her daddy saw new possibilities.

Everyone said God knows she tried
but what could you expect
from a man with no class at all,
and some worried about how the children
would turn out
but she was from a good family
and was a hard-working mother.
Money was scarce and after a while
so were her healthy days,
heart trouble, they said,
and long times not able to work.
But she did not complain
even when the children grew up and moved out,
and if she ever thought about her soldier
she did not say.

Some said her life was small
and she must have been lonely
and how could she have kept going,
but she did not ask these questions,
busy as she was
going to church when she felt up to it,
watching the TV,
helping her mother and daddy in their age,

sitting sometimes on that same porch
across the road from where
the schoolhouse had been—
now a flat spot so barren
that no one could ever imagine
there had been children
and games
and laughter
and bells.

◆ ◆ ◆

Funeral For A Gentle Person

Behind the coffin,
flowing from the pews,
brother, sister, children, grandchildren, cousins, aunts,
a river of kinship bears her
to a place we hope she dreamed about,
all those days alone
in a small house
by the side of a busy road,
no cars stopping.

◆ ◆ ◆

Life After Mississippi

I

The question always hanging
behind my head is
"Can I make it to Mississippi?"
Every old car I've looked at and bought,
"Will this baby make it to Mississippi?"
Every tank of gas
will almost get me back to Mississippi.
Every paycheck has to be enough
at least for a bus ticket
even though I don't want to go.
Long ago I could have stopped worrying,
but now it could be war
or the great depression
or cancer
sending me back into the family land,
where I'd walk through a woodsy bottom,
a world as far away as it used to be,
and I would garden and hunt
and fish clean streams,
and eat catfish and bream with no spots in their flesh,
and store onions and potatoes in a root cellar,
and be a neighbor to everyone
for as long as we lasted.

II

I know a crease between the hills
where water comes from under a rock.
A little digging
and I'd have a spring
where I would take my bucket to fill every day
and leave a gourd so others could drink.

III

Sooner or later
the snake would come
but this time things would be different.
I would let him coil
in the top of that fallen pine,
his hourglass markings dark as death,
and against everything I've ever been taught,
would step around him,
no rock, no stick, no gun,
just staying alive in Mississippi.

◆ ◆ ◆

III. Mississippi Scrapbook

• • •

We lived close to the rhythms of life in Mississippi. We knew when the babies were born. We knew who was sick and who was dying. We hunted and fished, we played the games we taught ourselves, we explored the woods and found secret places. And in the center of it all was the family and the community and the church. The photographs in this section capture and share some of those rhythms. At left, Rev. Ewart A. and Lola Mae Autry and son Jerry, who died when he was 17. At right, Martha Lynn Autry (now Crawford) with older brother Jerry and their catch. Below, Ewart, the twins Martha Lynn and Lanny, and Jimmy (the author) in the big poplar tree deep in the woods.

We called it grabblin', and big fish were the reward, but grabblin' was as much a social event and a boy's rite of passage as anything else. When threatened, a catfish will make a rumbling sound, and the man who hears him will call, "I hear him thundering!" At right, a group of men probe a large drift of logs in the river—a sure bedding place for the big fish. But will there be a fish, or a snake, or a snapping turtle? At left, Martha Lynn and a neighbor and a prize fish. Below, three "good old boys," including Uncle Everson Autry (center). Out of the river the fish is helpless, but in chest-deep water he could drown any man foolish enough to put a hand in that mouth.

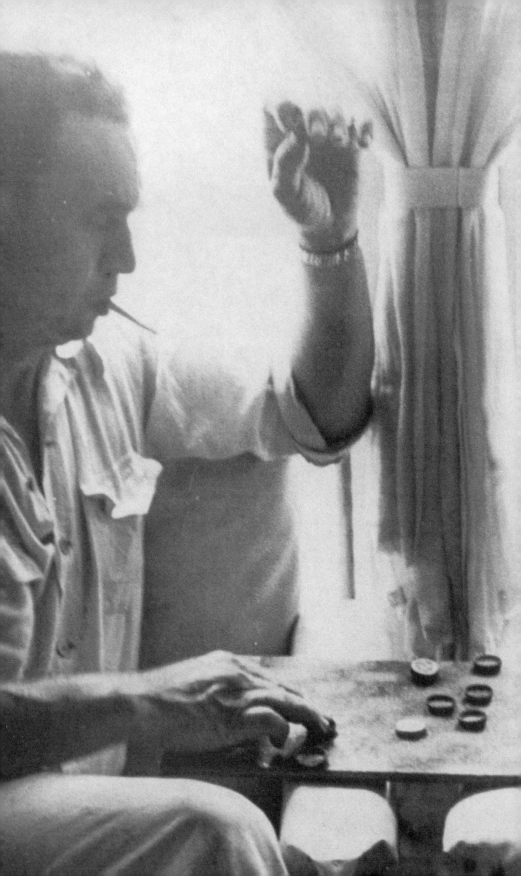

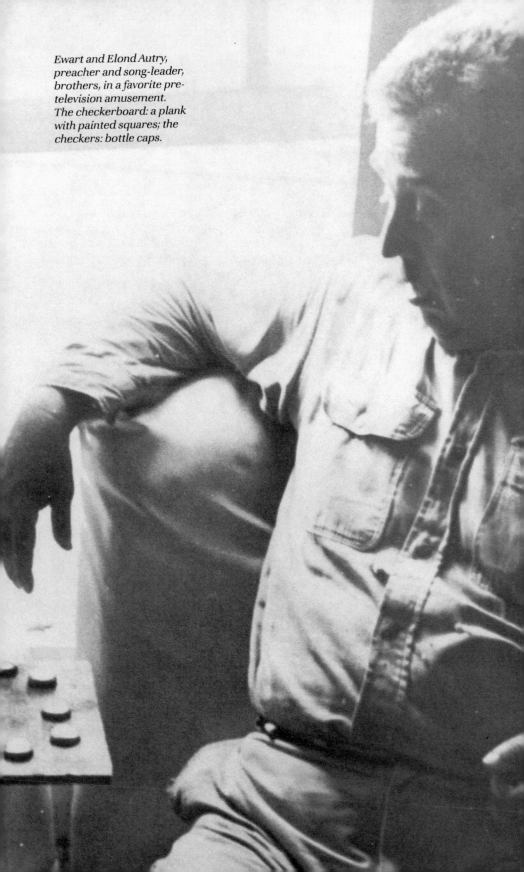

*Ewart and Elond Autry,
preacher and song-leader,
brothers, in a favorite pre-
television amusement.
The checkerboard: a plank
with painted squares; the
checkers: bottle caps.*

Then there was plain old fishing, with poles, lines, hooks, and bait. The first photograph in this book (page 2) is of Aunt Mary Eliza Hudspeth and the fish she caught on her 90th birthday. At left, Lanny and a "grinnell." Below, Ewart and a big snapper. At right, a neighbor wading out among the fish.

Animals, even insects, were valuable everyday parts of our lives. We hunted with dogs and plowed with mules. In turn we cared for their needs, and they became like members of the family. At left, Lanny with a faithful foxhound; Below, Jerry and Jimmy in a sled drawn by old Joe. At right, Lanny and Martha Lynn in the excitement of a "Betsy Bug Chariot Race"—match boxes pulled by bugs in harnesses of thread.

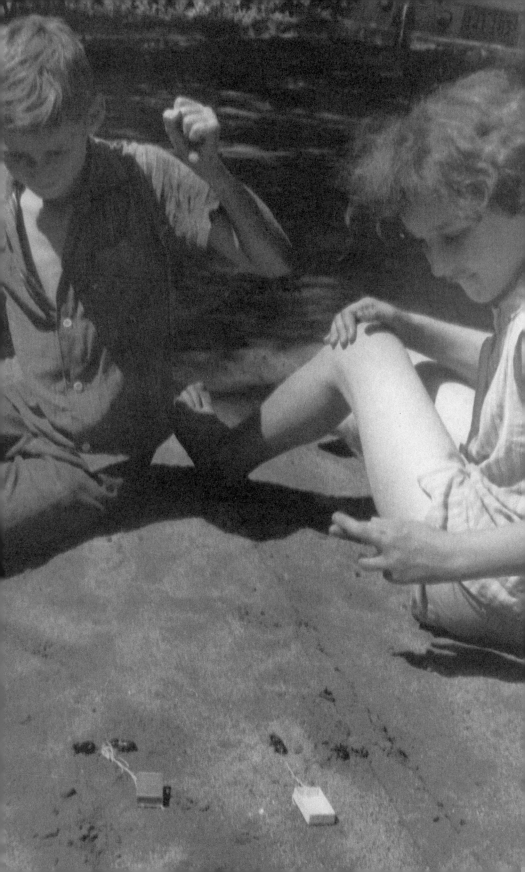

Political campaigns were more benign and considerably more entertaining in those days. The people gave the candidates time and a place to visit. While the "gossip center" at left was done in good humor, the people came to listen seriously—though some speeches, even then, were dull enough to make the babies sleep. Below, men and boys sit at Abel's store, practicing the lost art of watching the cars go by.

The church was the center of the community in earlier years and was the source of its own special stories. At left is Pine Grove Church where, as the story was often told, a Yankee patrol came and, leaving weapons outside, worshipped with the children and old people who made up the congregation during the war. In this cemetery are Civil War graves still clearly marked. Below, Ewart Autry, longtime pastor of Pine Grove; in the background is a picture of his father, Rev. James A. Autry, also pastor of Pine Grove in the early years of this century. At right, Ewart baptizes Jerry, his son, in the Tippah River.

Hunting meant food first, sport second. The rule in most families was "kill to eat, and eat what you kill," the only exceptions being poisonous snakes and varmints that preyed on chickens and small livestock. Above, Jerry (at left) and Lanny (second from right) and friends at the end of a rabbit hunt. At right, a proud Cousin Douglas Autry and his buck. At left, a possum up a tree.

From the time people first cut roads through the woods of north Mississippi or cleared a path for fences or power lines, the rains, with no undergrowth to slow the water, would wash away the soil. We thought kudzu would stop all that. To some extent it did, but nothing has been able to stop the kudzu. It smothers out thousands of acres of trees every year, and as it grows and climbs everything in its path, it takes on eerie shapes, as in the photo at left. Below, it reclaims for nature an abandoned house.

At right, a tree deep in the Autry woods, dubbed by Ewart as "nature's totem pole."

No one bought bait from a handy bait shop. There were three ways to get it: 1) catch insects like crickets or cockroaches or grasshoppers, 2) dig for worms or grubs or "ground puppies" (salamanders), or 3) seine for small fish or crawfish or other water creatures. Here, seining for bait in Autry Creek are Jerry, Lanny, Martha Lynn, and Ewart.

The dramatic photograph at right is of an Autry friend and neighbor and hunting companion, Mr. C. A. Falkner, with his "Judas crow," which he trained to call other crows. When they came, Mr. C.A. would shoot them.

At left, Ewart measures a big poplar tree, one of the few not cut years ago for lumber.

Below, the Tippah River, around which much life flowed. We fished in it, grabbled in it, swam in it, baptized in it, picnicked on its banks. We planted crops in the fields, which the river, with disheartening frequency, would then flood and ruin. The channeling of the Tippah stopped the regular floods and put much land into crop production—but it also put an end to the river's central role in our lives.

IV. Paying Attention

• • •

Photograph by Sally Pederson

New Birth
for Sally
Spring, 1984

From her sure knowledge
that everything would come out all right,
things began to come out all right,
out through the present day horrors,
through my fears and loss and grief,
through the demons lurking around everything I do.

As if directly from that optimism,
Ronald came unconcerned into the cold and light,
no longer surrounded by the sounds of Sally's life,
but sliding easily into the doctor's bloody hands
then snuggling back onto his mother's warmth,
none of his father's wailing against the world,
none of that waiting for the next shoe to fall.

And I count toes and fingers
and check his little penis
and touch the soft spot on his head
and watch the doctor probe and squeeze,
not believing everything came out all right.

Later I wonder how these years have come
from pain to death to pain to life
to what next?
A baby babbling in the backpack,
a mother walking her healthy pace,
a dog trailing behind,
and me holding on,
through the neighborhood, through everything,
with each day
one by one
coming out all right.

◆ ◆ ◆

On Paying Attention

There came a time in my volunteer life
when I began to give in
to the seductions of righteousness
and to think of my work as a sacrifice
for the good of others.
I would make schedules no one should try
so that people would ask
how it was possible for one man to do so much.
It was a time of three speeches
and three cities
in one day,
and in all the scurrying
I did not want the delay
of a restroom conversation
with a hesitant little man
in a cheap new suit.
I needed a quick pee, five minutes to think,
and two minutes to get to the podium.
But there he was,
with the side effects I knew so well,
the puffy cheeks, the swollen gums
as he smiled and told me he had a job now
and hadn't had a seizure in six months.
I gave him the quick back pat
and the smile,
never expecting to see him again.
But he sat in the front row
and smiled a greeting when I rose to speak,
the dignitary from the national office,
bringing word from Washington,
the National Commission,
the Hill, the White House.
He smiled too often
and over-nodded and made too much of his notes,
clicking his pen and turning pages,
back and forth,
as if studying what he'd written.
When our eyes met he smiled and nodded,
another guy, I thought, who wants people
to think he knows the speaker.
So I avoided looking at him

until he shuffled, crossed his legs,
and stretched them in front of him.
When I saw the soles of his shoes,
slightly soiled, less than a day worn,
I realized he had bought the suit and shoes
just for this meeting,
just to hear a speech squeezed
into an afternoon between two other cities.
He had looked forward to it,
planned for it,
put new job money into it,
and would make notes
so that he could remember always
what the important man came to teach.

But the lesson was mine to learn—
about sacrifice
and counting blessings,
about patience
and paying attention to teachers
wherever I find them.

◆ ◆ ◆

Airport Scene I.

She had country girl written all over her,
except on her T-shirt
which said "I'm terrific,"
but I know she never said terrific
until she came to the city
and went to secretary school
and learned to dress and make up
then got a job
and tried to be terrific
enough to marry a new salesman
now getting off a plane
on Friday night,
too tired for the baby on her hip
and wondering if his wife's body
will ever be terrific again.

◆ ◆ ◆

Airport Scene II.

It used to be train stations
but now it's airports,
the core sample of humanity,
rushing always and waiting,
crying hellos and goodbyes.
Think about that,
how high and fast they go,
machines full of people,
miracle rays guiding them everywhere on earth,
billions of dollars of invisible signals
bringing the people down safely
so they can rush and wait
and cry their hellos and goodbyes,
just like in the train stations.

◆ ◆ ◆

Airport Scene III.

I know a traveler in a hurry,
always fidgeting in the rampway,
who wants to paint a red line
on the floor at every gate
and announce "No hugging or kissing
before you reach the red line"
so other people,
especially him,
won't be delayed by all that affection.

◆ ◆ ◆

Airport Scene IV.

Infants they say have a special filter
that shuts down the hearing
when the world gets too loud,
letting them sleep through
jack hammers or rock and roll,
an enviable gift, I think,
rushing through an airport,
but reserved for infants
because they would not be able
to deal with the noise,
and would scream
at the engines
and metal announcements
and whistles and horns.

But when the body grows
we hear it all
whether we can deal with it or not,
a random thought,
seeing a retarded woman in the crosswalk,
admist the horns and whistles and yells,
her father at her side,
her eyes moving without focus,
her body jerking against the noise,
like a shot rabbit against the pellets,
but the father squeezing and patting,
his head close,
pouring his "okay" and "good" and "almost there"
into her ear,
love filtering the noise.

◆ ◆ ◆

Widow

She told the children
they didn't have to keep going to the same church,
they could take their children to a bigger church,
with a gym and a pool,
not reminding them their father was still
fertilizing the azaleas
where he had been scattered,
white dust on a rainy day,
drifting under the black umbrellas
after we dug our hands into the urn
and broadcast him
like seed
among the flowers
then walked to the cars
and noticed him
like talcum
on our shoes and around our cuffs,
and later found he had come home with us,
under our fingernails,
then before supper
scrubbed with those little stiff bristle brushes
and tried to wash him away.

◆ ◆ ◆

Listening To Old Wounds

A man I love is going crazy
they say,
but he says it's only his hearing.

   Get a hearing aid, I say

and he says,

   Then people shout at you.

And I say,

   I am shouting.

He knows the truth
but tells me he used to have good ears,

   I could hear a whine on the line
   a hundred yards away.
   Knew just which pole to climb.

and that the Japs ruined his hearing
in New Guinea,
the night they parachuted
right on top of his unit,
silent among the foxholes,
all of them lost in the dark,
shouting passwords and trusting no one.

   I had to listen too hard
   that night. A twig cracking.
   Anything.

After the fighting he sat
for weeks
pounding an Australian coin with
a soup spoon
until the coin became a ring
which he sent me,
too big then
but which I wore for years.
Now he doesn't remember the ring,
and when I mention it
he cocks his head and squints,
as if listening for the memory,
but he hears only

"them damn jabbering yellow monkeys"
drifting above him,

>   *They didn't know*
>   *we were down there and we couldn't tell*
>   *where the voices were coming from.*

then dropping among his buddies,
the shooting and screaming,
the silence,
life depending on his ears.

I can understand why they say
he's going crazy.
It has something to do with all the sounds,
heartbeats, footsteps, breathing,
out there somewhere,
who knows how far away,
but still listened for—
still listened for.

◆ ◆ ◆

Madrap**
for Jimmy

This is a place of daily miracles
where strangers sit in circles
and discover the lost language of love,
putting themselves back together,
fitting tears and anger and pain
like puzzle pieces
until their stories make sense again.

◆ ◆ ◆

**
Mercy Alcohol and Drug Rehabilitation Program, M.A.D.R.P.,
pronounced "Madrap" by those in the program.

Hospital Visits

Under my arm is a blue folder
stuffed with everything I could ever learn
about booze and dope
except how to feel when
sitting in a circle with other children
it comes his turn and he says
"I'm Jim, an alcoholic and drug addict."

Next to me in the elevator is a couple with a pillow
for sitting on the floor
in a circle with other couples
learning to strain and grunt and breathe
another child into birth.

In the slow and acrid elevator
I want to tell them everything
about how it never ends,
being a parent,
about how it transforms you forever,
beyond celebration or pain or death.

But this is not the time or place
for a born again father to make his speech,
so I say "good luck"
and pray safe deliverance for us all.

◆ ◆ ◆

Baptism

There's something about this,
about putting the people under the water
and raising them up
in the name of the Father, the Son, and the Holy Ghost,
something that makes the people cry,
that makes them want to want
everything to be all right,
that makes them want to leave this place
and be better,
to immerse themselves in their lives
and somehow be washed clean
of all the things they think
they should not have done
and should not still want to do.
That's it.
Not the other stuff,
the star in the east,
the treasures in heaven,
or any of the old stories.
Not even life after death.
It is only to be new again.

◆ ◆ ◆

Present Day Horrors

The present day horrors
would be bad enough in themselves,
abstractly,
but it's the little scenes of desperation and despair
playing through everything
that finally get us:
A kleenex full of phlegm

> *Save that. Don't throw it away.*
> (I won't.)
> *They don't believe I cough up stuff.*
> *Save it. Show them.*
> (I will.)

And the nurse comes and I give it to her
with all the urgency I can feign

> *See?*
> *They said there was nothing there.*

And he grins and nods
knowing they will believe him now.

Later I see a tiny light of recognition
after the lung collapses and I come
in the midst of the struggle
wondering how and when it will end
watching that wild stare over the respirator mask
seeing all the energy go with every breath,
none to spare for the hello nod,
only enough for one more breath,
and one more.

Then someone says

> *When the eyes get dry it's over.*

and I wonder what that means
watching the eyes dryer and dryer
until something very small changes
and I think

> *Shit he's not here now.*
> *He's not staying for this part.*

the spaces between breaths growing

until that's all there is.

And that last space fills with memories
of little struggles in the middle of the night,
of incoherent sentences
like "oh why now pee"
and I hold his penis and point it into the bedpan
as he used to hold mine those years ago
when he was the adult and I was the child.
And he is embarrassed
and I am embarrassed for him
but we smile,
a last signal that after all this
we're still together
through these little scenes,
through the phlegm
and urine and blood and oxygen
and hypos and IVs,
through every pun and every game
and every old joke,
right up to the lung-crushing eye-drying end.

◆ ◆ ◆

The Wig

It was as if he had not even tried
for a match,
the way the ads promise,
using real human hair
to match what was there before,
and we didn't know what to say
when he limped into the office,
then he laughed,
"Hell, with the doctor bills,
who can afford a decent rug?"
and we realized it was his last big joke.
One day the wig was short, another long,
then he changed colors,
then blacked a tooth,
"always clowning," we would say later,
shaking our heads and smiling,
"right up to the end."
But as usual we missed the point,
about how people pay more attention to a clown
than to a dying man.

◆ ◆ ◆

Camping Memories

Surrounded by a deep and warm night
we breathed into each other's hair.
Life moved around us and between us,
creatures and feelings waked and stirred
making quiet and simple sounds.
There were no predators.
Reptiles did not bite
and insects did not sting.

◆ ◆ ◆

In John Maguire's Garden

Claremont, May 15, 1988

Very formal in places
because some people need the predictability,
this garden still has wild spots which draw me,
like a raucous chorus of Amazing Grace
late after some distinguished dinner,
or an eyebrow twisting upward
below a mortar board,
unexpected, distracting, beyond cultivation.

Some might hurry to prune the overgrown places,
to soften the surprise
of coming upon life so extravagant
that it outblooms the boundaries.
But not me, John,
not me.
I believe the gardener knew what he was doing.

◆ ◆ ◆

Reminiscence At Toul
July 18, 1987

Thirty years ago
on New Year's eve
drunk on French champagne
we shot bottle rockets
from the windows
of Hank and Willi's
rented chateau overlooking Nancy.

It sounds so worldly
which is how we wanted to think of ourselves,
but Lord, we were just children,
sent by the government to fly airplanes
and to save western Europe
from World War III.

We thought we had all the important things
still left to do
and were just playing at importance
for the time being.
It never occurred to us,
living in our community of friends,
having first babies,
seeing husbands die,
helping young widows pack to go home,
that we had already started the important things.
What could we have been thinking,
or perhaps it's how could we have known
that times get no better,
that important things come without background music,
that life is largely a matter of paying attention.

◆ ◆ ◆

Tannois

for Adam Growald
July 21, 1987, aboard The Princess

At the *lavois*
down the hill from her house
she tells about the day
she saved the Americans from the rain,
two men, two women, and a child,
un petit garcon,
nineteen months old the mother said,
on bicycles in the rain,
and she tells how they came in
and how they loved her dog and cats and doves.
It was in the summer of 1987
and they came on bicycles
from a boat on the canal,
in the rain,
and stopped under her eaves
and she invited them in.
And the others listen,
having heard it before,
and shake their heads
about Americans riding bicycles in the rain.

How large it seemed to her
in the smallness of her kitchen
with its backless chairs and curtainless windows,
in the smallness of her village,
where foreigners come through,
sometimes in tanks and sometimes on bicycles,
sometimes to make war
and sometimes to come in out of the rain.

Years from now a boy will look at a snapshot.
His mother will say,
your Uncle Jim took this the day
we got caught in the rain,
and this old French lady,
see her in the shadows there,
invited us into her home.
The boy will smile at the picture,
but he can never believe
that in a village in France,
among old ladies gathered at the *lavois*,
there still is talk of how
their friend once saved the Americans from the rain.

◆ ◆ ◆

Life In America

There's a line I want to use,
see?
in a poem I want to write,
okay?
Now don't groan or roll your eyes.
Give me a break.
I mean, hey, give it a chance
to grow on you,
okay?
It's a line I thought of,
watching some guys after a golf game
drinking in the club house
and slapping cards on the table
and checking their watches and saying
like, you know, "oh hell,
about time to go home or my old lady'll
give me a load of shit."
This line is about those guys
plus a lot of other people,
let me tell you,
people in loud dance places,
standing around the floor,
checking out the action,
if you know what I mean.
And people in bowling alleys,
okay?
yelling at the pins and each other.
This line,
and believe me, I wrote it myself,
I swear I never heard it before,
this line is about all those people I see
and not just those,
others,
at restaurants and ball games
and even at church.
It's a line about how they act
and in a way it's a line about America.
But hey, I don't want to get too heavy,
you know?
I just want to say this one little line

and let you take it from there,
okay?
Hey look, seriously, the line is
(are you ready for this?)
"living lives of boisterous desperation."
Lives of boisterous desperation.
How about that?
Not *quiet* desperation, like the other guy wrote
about another time and another place,
but *boisterous* desperation.
Get it?
Get it?
Sure you do.

◆ ◆ ◆

The Story Of The Beginning
Of The End Of The World

It was a time when many people had the answers.
Some sold the answers
to other people who came
on weekends to listen and
nod and hug each other and
sometimes scream and sometimes
take off their clothes and
always say "thank you for sharing."

Some sold the answers
in books about feeling better and
taking charge of your life and
walking a new path and
discovering many zones and spots
you never knew you had
in your head or on your body.

Some sold the answers
in church with quotations about
giving and receiving and
which one is always better and
warnings about finding the answers in
books or from false prophets
who abounded in times like these.

Some sold the answers
in business schools and in stock markets,
in union halls and in capitals of government
and, for those of lesser means,
in blind alleys and back stairways
and places where other people
wouldn't even think to look for the answers.

◆ ◆ ◆

Leo

He threw water on my motorcycle's one sparkplug
so I wouldn't be able to leave him,
so I would have to stay,
his buddy,
and play in the back yard,
the only place he was allowed to go.

Early before anyone was up
he would fill a tumbler with tap water
then sneak out the front door
of his side of the duplex
and tiptoe to where the Harley 125 was chained
and pour a little puddle around the plug.

Later, late and frustrated,
drying the plug, grease on my hands,
I would yell at him

> *Goddammit, Leo, you're making me late*
> *I've got to go to school.*

and sometimes chase him and pretend
I was going to hit him.
But he would only repeat what he said
every morning of every day of every year
we lived in that duplex

> *You Leo's buddy*
> *Play with Leo now.*

Leo would stand,
his big droopy frame shutting out the light
from the back screen door,
and watch mother cook.

> *Rufe play with Leo?*

His breathing was noisy
and he sometimes drooled
and his eyes looked in different directions.
Mother would say "that big dumb thing
scares me and I wish they'd keep him
off the back porch,"
and I would say "if he's so dumb
how does he know to ground out my sparkplug."

We knew his age and his mind's age
and we knew they'd didn't match,
but we didn't know anything else
except he was Italian
and his big family kept him there with them,
in the duplex,
and they had barbecues in the back yard
and drank beer and laughed with each other,
and that Leo played on the ground
with the other children
like a big pet, I thought.
And they all seemed happy enough.

I hadn't thought about Leo in years, of course,
until just the other day,
just after the tests were in,
just after the pediatrician
in his I am your friend voice
said something to us like,
"Well, he'll never go to Harvard Medical School,
but he'll be very functional
and will be able to do a lot of things."

Later, I wondered if that meant things like
ground out a sparkplug with a glass of water
or play the family pet
with children a third his age.

And I thought,
sometimes God makes you write things on the blackboard
a thousand times.

◆ ◆ ◆

Distractions

It was a matter of distraction;
I could not hear my baby sons,
those struggling years ago,
in a trailer or an apartment
or old house where I thought
money was the problem
and did not want to be distracted
by the babbling of children.
Or it could have been the constrictions,
of a trailer, an apartment, an old house, a cockpit
or an office with two other people
and no way to stand out
but to put my head down and work
so hard I could not afford
to be constricted by children.

But this is not the same old cry of guilt,
the if-only-I-had-another-chance,
because after all these years
a chance came,
another son,
this time with me ready to listen.
But he is distracted,
something about constrictions in his brain
making him busy inside himself,
with so much to do
that he talks to himself
more than to me,
and every day I try to persuade him
to live in this world
and to let me know he's with me
if only from time to time.

◆ ◆ ◆

Poet's Prayer

If I write another poem
let it be about love,
not the crazy love
we all start out writing about
but the love that keeps us sane,
the love that pain reveals
at a funeral
or when the doctor says what we don't want to hear;
the love that men won't talk about,
of work, of games, of one another;
the love of divorced people
when they find their way back to marriage;
the love of an old family place
when the generations gather there;
the love of old friends
who realize they're the only ones left;
and the love of children,
not only when they're smiling or sleeping
or clean or straight or strong or smart,
but when they are none of those things
and need more love than anyone can give,
and cannot even recognize the love they get.

◆ ◆ ◆

Matters Of The Heart

*(On the Lear, after learning of a
blocked coronary artery, 4/20/80)*

What makes the heart stop?

> On the Lear the heart stops
> when the noise stops
> or the CAT strikes.

What about the flatbed truck?

> Then too,
> Chigger trying to jump the ditch
> behind the road machine
> or hit it,
> on the way to Wolf River
> where the yellow water tried to suck me under.

And the motorcycle?

> *Yes, I twisted the handlebar*
> *pushing myself at the heart's edge*
> *with the fear in seconds,*
> *spinning and tumbling on the muddy road.*

What then of the cancer?

> It did not happen to me.

Didn't it?

> It was the heart, remember?

But wasn't your heart connected to his cancer?

> And to many things.

So what really makes the heart stop?

> No one knows,
> but I know this:
> it practices and practices.

◆ ◆ ◆

Christmas In New York

Don't let *Adeste Fideles* near a tenor sax
or else
some gaunt music major
will beat it to death for tuition.
At Bloomie's the Salvation Army lady
carols on a baritone horn,
and a fey young man listens,
tiny jingle bells in a pierced ear.
On the church steps the Fifth Avenue Four
urge themselves onward
through the *Saints*,
from the music stamped
"Property of Juilliard,"
perfectly,
which is not how it is to be played.

Could I take my sax
and fake it through Christmas on a corner?
Not the music but the rest of it,
the youth
the cold
the needs
the hope
the feeling it hasn't passed me by,
or vice versa?

◆ ◆ ◆

Homeless Saxophonist

I can tell from his riffs
he is not on Lexington Avenue,
leaning against Grand Central,
his fingers our only proof he's still alive.
We are here,
stepping around his feet,
pushing our way uptown,
his notes wild against the taxi horns.
But he is not playing where we are;
he is in another place,
a dark place small and crowded,
where people are smiling and shaking their heads
in that funny way real jazz fans have,
and there is a bass
and drums
and piano,
always with him, steady as dirt,
chords leading to just where he wants his sax to take him,
farther away still,
to a place he has not yet been
but will know the first time he feels it.

◆ ◆ ◆

Why Men Fly

We sat around waiting
to see who had lit up the desert,
each of us with somebody
we did not want it to be,
burning out there,
coyotes and pack rats,
bright-eyed by the fire,
running jumping onto and around
rags of hot metal
scattered a mile,
nibbling perhaps at the odd chunks of meat.

All of us wondered the same thing
as each number landed,

> *Apache four two is in*
> *Apache one eight is in*

as each head-shaking, wet-suited man
came in counting the chairs,
checking each face for the missing one.

We did not know that melodrama
worked against us
until a cajun boy hit his fist
on the table and sobbed,
"Why didn't they get out?"
And one of the instructors
hand-picked a bunch of us into another room
and said
"Anybody who can't take this without crying
better quit now."
Then as we tried variations on stony faced,
he said,
"After all, if flying were safe,
why the hell do it?"

◆ ◆ ◆

Flying Safety Lesson

They said it was a lesson
about oxygen management,
then came a tape of radio talk,
an incident they called it,
involving a flight of four F-100s
from the States to Spain
with a stop in the Azores,
beginning with those voices you've heard
in the flying movies,

> "Check in, Red Four."
> "Roger."
> The Roger doesn't sound right,
> slurred,
> so the leader says "Oxygen check,"
> but by then it is already too late,
> and Red Four mumbles.

We knew why they wanted us to hear the tape,
something about fear,
about checking oxygen,
about things not to do
like starve our brains and dive into the sea,
old stuff we knew already.
But the mumble
made our necks tingle,
weeks later listening.

> The leader says, "Three, check out Red Four."
> Red Four says nothing,
> then Red Three shouts,
> "Pull up, Red Four, you're diving.
> Pull up, pull up."

We did not look at one another
but picked at our fingernails
or doodled or stared at the tape player.
Later we would discuss oxygen management
and safety checks
and all the routines that became so routine
between the Azores and Spain
that they didn't get done.

> Then comes the radar controller's voice,
> steady, commanding,
> "Red Four, this is Racecar Radar,

turn heading one three five degrees,"
then scared,
"Sir...Red Four Sir...please
turn right...now...heading one four zero degrees."
Then Red Three drops the call sign,
"Bob, please listen to me,
pull up, level your wings,
look at me, wave, give me a sign,
say something."

Then the mumble,
trying hard we thought,
but too late the Flight Surgeon told the class,
"His brain was gone by that time, Gentlemen."

Now the tape plays a lot of silence.
Red Three says, "Bob, please pull up,
pull back on the stick, ease back on the stick."
And the radar man asks "Altitude?"
And Red Three says, "five thousand and descending,"
and the radar man says
"Red Four...sir...please turn right...
please pull up."
And Red Three says,
his voice breaking at the edges,
"Bob look at me, wave, pull up."
Silence,
a shout, "No Bob, pull up, pull up."
More silence.
"Too late, too late."
And the radar man gives the coordinates
and the tape shuts off.

I don't remember the words the instructors chose
to restate the obvious,
but I remember the lesson they never intended,
about how technology fails
and humanity is the only thing left,
which sometimes is not enough.

◆ ◆ ◆

Examining The Wreckage

I am drawn to plane crashes.
I read about them,
every detail,
and try to figure out what happened
and what the pilot did wrong,
which is only a way of wondering what I would have done.

And of course I would have done it right,
have analyzed the problem,
the sputtering engine,
the heavy controls,
the failed generator,
and I would have gotten down okay,
and I would never have flown in that weather,
and I would have watched for ice,
and I would have turned back,
and I would never have gone near that thunderstorm
or flown those mountains at night
or taken a single engine over water
or any of those dumb things
other pilots do every day.

But when I think about the pilot years
I remember things done wrong:
an aileron roll too close to the ground,
a foggy landing I should not have tried,
a thunderstorm full of hail
like the sound of a thousand hammers,
a failed drag chute, a blown tire
and a bomb under the wing.
All that without a crash.

At this point I should make a metaphor
about life and flying,
but flying is easier than life.
When a plane crashes,
I can go there and know
that I am not in the wreckage.

◆ ◆ ◆

Jeopardy

I

How many times have I died?
At least once on the motorcycle,
with Jack Spencer on the back,
the unexpected cars
and the boy on the bicycle
and nothing to do but skid and hope.
Or run off the road
by the Cadillac passing on the hill
outside Holly Springs.
And certainly in the F-86
over the cotton fields below Rabat
with Dickie on the radio

> *Jesus, Cowboy, pull up before you roll!*

(Think of that,
of all the hoeing and picking,
of all the sun hot hours in cotton fields,
to hang my wing
and tumble into pieces
on some foreigner's cotton
ten thousand miles from my people's land.)

And in the fog at Wethersfield
in an Englishman's pasture
with sheep like gray boulders
in a wash of green
only a hundred yards from the runway
but far enough that all I could say
was Oh Shit.

And in the whistling silence
of a dead engine.
And in a thunderstorm
that rolled back and wrinkled the metal skin
like an old time cigarette paper.
And in a hundred things I didn't even know about.

II

There are courts of inquiry somewhere,
accident investigators piecing it together.
There are coroners,
there are undertakers trying to make me
look okay after all.
There are caskets shipped back
filled with rubber sacks
not nearly full enough.
There are honor guards clicking their heels
and firing rifles in country cemeteries.
There are proud mothers
and wet-eyed widows
and children with pictures for fathers.

III

But through all those deaths,
I am here,
still and again,
with at least one to go,
and the only thing changed
is the limb I am out on.

◆ ◆ ◆

ABOUT THE AUTHOR

James A. Autry, the son and grandson of Mississippi Baptist ministers, spent much of his growing up time among the hills and hollows of Benton County, Mississippi. There, under the influence of the people of Pine Grove Church and the Abel's Store community, he learned the rituals and values and sense of community that passed from generation to generation.

After Autry graduated from the University of Mississippi, he served as a jet fighter pilot in the Air Force. Then he entered the newspaper business and moved from there to *Better Homes and Gardens*.

Much of his poetry was written on airliners in which he spends many hours a year in his present job as President of the Magazine Group of Meredith Corporation, publishers of *Better Homes and Gardens* and other magazines.

Autry and his wife, Sally Pederson, and their six-year-old son, Ronald, live in Des Moines, Iowa.

ABOUT THE PHOTOGRAPHER

Lola M. Autry was born in Memphis, Tennessee. She was educated in the city schools and received a B.S. degree from Memphis State University. She has written articles for national magazines, as well as having had many photographs published. She is author of one book and co-author of two others with her husband. She owns her own photographic studio. In addition, she is choir director and organist at her church.

The Autry home is deep in the woods among the high hills of North Mississippi, nine miles from the nearest town. She says, "I would have it no other way!"